SILENCE IS NOT A STRATEGY

BY
Stephanie Myers

Contents

Prologue

Why are many women silent in front of the men they work with? More women are working in male-dominated professions each year and our numbers appear to be growing…but at what costs? Look at this quick read before you answer: Women in Male-Dominated Industries and Occupations (Quick Take). If we want our numbers to increase more, we will have to speak up more and share our brilliance and ingenuity. So why aren't some of us speaking more? Why aren't you? What are you afraid of (fill in the blank with your best answer)? Being outnumbered can make some women keep quiet and it can be quite intimidating. There are so many men at work, plus not all of them are there to lend support. There is always the possibility of being made to look like an idiot when we do speak up. Who wants to be ridiculed for having a different solution to a problem? No one. What woman do you know desires not to have her suggestions taken seriously? Then, as quiet as it is kept, there is always the added fear of some type of payback or retribution, like getting fired, or unjustifiably not getting the promotion when we do stand up and speak our truth. These are some harsh examples but they are enough for women to keep their lips closed and play along like everything is all right. If you recognize this woman, please tell her that she does not have to play around with bias on any level. She can learn what it takes to speak up like the informed woman who has earned her spot at the grownup's table!

In 2024, women are still subjected to stereotypical behavior that makes it seemingly impossible for us to succeed on a large scale. This is terrible! Have you ever wondered why the numbers stay so low for women working in the C-suites of Fortune 500 companies? Our numbers are increasing, yes, but they are still too low. This study provides reasons why so few women make it to the very top: that rarefied air of being the top executive in charge of a major organization [Women in the Workplace Study](). We are so happy when a woman finally gets to be the boss and take the helm! Even against a backdrop of harmful stereotypes and unfavorable working environments, women have made and continue to make strides toward equity. Now is not the time to keep quiet and shy away from bias.

Let's face it: some of us simply refuse (or rather choose) not to speak up when the answer to our company's problems may be held between our lips. As stated earlier, there can be a litany of reasons why women do not speak up. Why we will not share our expertise and unique way of doing things with our male coworkers is a travesty all on its own. This book takes a glimpse inside some of the more familiar reasons why women may think it is harmless just to keep their mouths closed when actually "Silence is not a Strategy!"

ABOUT THE AUTHOR

Hi, my name is Stephanie Myers. I have worked in various male-dominated occupations for over 25 years. During this time, I have experienced my share of biases working with men. Not all men, to be clear, but enough male-centered, male-focused biases that made my work life much harder than it should have been. I have never been a woman who "holds back" when asked my opinion and I speak in a direct tone of voice to everyone. My tone is a problem for some men, mainly because so many want to dish it out (being direct) towards women but can't handle it when it is handed right back to them! Anyway, I will speak more about my adventures working in male-dominated professions later in our journey. Yes, I now refer to my struggles as a journey because I triumphed over those experiences and learned a great deal about myself in the process. Like many of you, as a woman working in a male-dominated sector of the workforce, I am still on a journey toward true equity in the workplace. It saddens me to witness women become silent in front of their male peers. Women who have the same job title or college degree (if not more) as their male colleagues, yet find it uncomfortable to truly express their thoughts and ideas out loud….in front of the men. To be honest, such encounters make me uncomfortable for them and me (you know, the sisterhood).

I do realize that speaking up can come with a cost attached to it because women are still fighting for parity in so many areas of life. For some women, this price is too high to pay. Over my years of working in this type of industry, I have experienced numerous encounters with male coworkers that ranged anywhere from a demeaning slight when speaking to me to downright lying on me when a product was damaged and no one knew exactly who had done the deed, yet it was always directed toward me (I suppose they have to protect the brotherhood). If you take nothing else from this book, remember this one thing…keep your guard up until you truly know the people working around you. Understand not every pool of bias that you wade into will come from the guys you work with. Women can be biased towards other women in a male-dominated environment. Bias is a prejudice that can rear its head anywhere and appear in practically anyone, their title makes no difference. Dealing with management level bias is different than dealing with coworker bias simply because of the title and status given to management personnel. Fortunately, a company generally has a hierarchy for everyone to follow if an issue goes unresolved.

As I always say," My boss has a boss." I simply move up the chain of command and give my argument to what has taken place on the job. Be prepared when doing so because, depending on the mindset of those in authority, intimidation plays a huge part in why women tend to remain silent and not "trouble the waters." I have been blessed realizing that with each occurrence dealing with mid-level management, senior-level management was willing to listen to both sides of the argument and render a verdict (more on that topic later). My reason for writing this book is for women to pull back the curtain and see what it is that causes so many of us to clam up when we finally get a seat at the proverbial table and find ourselves with an opportunity to share our thoughts out loud. Once you're seated at the table…that means you've made it, right? Bias is no longer an issue that women have to contend with...right? Think back to how many female CEOs of Fortune 500 companies there are before you give a definite answer. I want to share some of my experiences when working with men on a day-to-day basis and how I overcame many of the obstacles that were intended to crush my spirit and "keep me in my place." You are not alone in your challenges to be seen, heard and respected. This is not a male-bashing book. I truly enjoy working with the majority of my male colleagues. The few men who did try to have me lose my cool only made me powerful in the long run. Your mindset and confidence in your own abilities have a great deal to do with overcoming misogynistic behavior. This book reveals what many women (I am not the only one) who work in what is still considered by many to be a "man's job" have to reckon with today and how those same women can learn to speak their truth without fear or sorrow for being equally competent to a man. If you are unclear regarding the word misogyny and what it entails, here is a read *from Verywell Mind* that provides a frame of reference for you to consider about your own work environment What is Misogyny?

This is important: I am not a therapist. I do understand the importance of getting psychological help if a person needs it. We do not go through life and perceive everything the same way. If feelings of inadequacy have placed you in a downward mood swing from your normal self and you cannot find your way back to center, please seek medical advice. I share my experiences with you in the hope that insight will be gained on how to handle certain situations at work better. My experiences may not be the exact same since we work different jobs, but they will be similar in nature. Many of you will resonate with what I am saying to you. I made it through my ordeals and I want to help you make it through yours. This book does not replace sound medical advice for those of you who feel like nothing will ever change and the bias at work is insurmountable. I believe that if I can manage the biases in my life, you can also manage it in yours. My ability to thrive in a male-dominated environment is what I share with you in the hope that your days can be fulfilling and not anxiety-ridden due to the biased behavior of others.

ACKNOWLEDGEMENTS

I dedicate this book to my mother, Mary Thompson Myers. I miss you, mommy. My mom taught me that using my voice and speaking up for myself regarding what is right and what is true are some of the best gifts a person can be given. I tend to agree. I also want to acknowledge and thank the women whose names we may never get to know. Women who waged war against bias while working in male-dominated occupations and never lost hope…despite what they had to endure. Never losing your insight for the bigger picture, our future generations, is what will make it easier for women to get ahead and be the leaders that we have always been. Once younger generations of women and girls see what can be achieved in any workplace, they will be content knowing whatever field of study, whatever job or position within an organization they may want to hold, the door is open for them.

The experiences shared in this book are my own. I share them in the spirit of giving and shedding light on some of the biases I faced during my journey and how I have come to manage bias without stress or a sense of inferiority. I pray, as you continue reading, there will be tips that can help you manage the bias you may be experiencing on the job as well.

CHAPTER 1

The Voice Within

"A woman with a voice is by definition a strong woman. But the search to find that voice can be remarkably difficult." – Melinda Gates

Finding your voice and having the willingness to use it is a challenge all by itself. As women, we can spend years concentrating on what to say and when to say it. Please be mindful of your tone! We don't want anyone to feel bad about something we have said to them. This winding road toward finding our voice and using it properly usually begins in our childhood. Depending on the type of parent that reared you, you may have been taught the adage "children are to be seen and not heard" or "don't speak unless spoken to." Either way, it just means to keep quiet (along with 'look cute' and 'try and stay clean'). Others may have been reared on the other side of the speaking continuum and had parents who wanted you to announce in a loud voice that you were entering the room and go ahead, "speak your mind so long as you do it respectfully". Then we grow up, leave home, meet up with friends, other coworkers, our potential mates and the rest is history. What I'm trying to point out is whether or not we put a voice to our thoughts has a lot to do with how we as look at ourselves and also how we were treated along the way toward womanhood. We reach adulthood with all its freedom and responsibilities…and then what? Do you, as a woman, speak up or hold your peace in the presence of men at work? Close your eyes and picture this… You are at a table with five male colleagues. You know the material being discussed very well. A question is asked, "Does anyone have any suggestions?" Do you (a) wait and let a man make the first suggestion, (b) just forget that you have a suggestion and look dumbfounded, or (c) speak up and tell everyone at the table your suggestion and why you think it is best. The answer most obviously depends on your personality. Different personalities react and do things in the way most comfortable for them.

I'm more focused on the answer (b) than the other two responses. There has to be a reason why a woman would "just forget" she has a suggestion or, even worse, knows the answer to whatever task or problem is of concern but does not speak up. What would be your reason for doing that if you were put in this situation? On many occasions, I have witnessed smart, educated (either by the streets, the books, or both) women just go blank when in the presence of men. Okay, many of us are talked over when we attempt to speak up and that experience shuts many of us down completely. Men know this, which is why many of them do it…to keep us quiet. If you work in a male-dominated industry there will be challenges to overcome. Are you ready to overcome them? I can show you ways to get around that particular situation. We don't have to put up with disrespect of any kind. Getting back to the woman who refused to share her answer…can this type of woman (her personality type) shake it off and get a grip on herself? Does she even want to shake it off? You know what I mean…shake off the fear. I confess there was a time when I did not speak up. I liked (had a crush on) a boy in my eighth-grade math class. One particular day, we were in math class and assigned into groups for problem-solving. I got to sit next to him! The math problem was put on the chalkboard and each group had to solve it and give their answer. Each group was huddled up in the team spirit of a "Solve the Math Problem Win a Prize" mentality. We took turns giving our solution to the problem. When it came to my love interest, he did not know the answer at all. Nothing, a complete blank. He truly did not know how to solve the problem. Guess what I did? For some reason, I didn't remember the answer either (I just did not want to speak up)! I mean, I couldn't make him look like he was dumb and I was smart. That wasn't ladylike plus, I wanted him to like me. The math class ended and of course my team lost. But I remember feeling a sense of disappointment within myself. It was on that day I decided never to allow a problem to go unanswered if I knew how to solve it…no matter who sat at the table. Fortunately, I have held to that standard since the eighth grade. That is how hard the disappointment within myself hit me. I still remember it to this day and never want to feel that way again. Has speaking up come with a price attached to it? Yes. Depending on who else is at the table, many women run the risk of not being supported at all for their work and creativity. Everyone is not an ally. Know the difference. Depending on the circumstance and the emotional IQ of the other person(s) involved, the price for speaking up in front of biased mentalities can be very steep. Most things that are truly worthwhile are going to cost you something in life. Do I think it is worth the cost? Most definitely, but that is just me. You will have to make up your mind about where and when you are going to draw that line in the sand and set a boundary.

CHAPTER 2

Despite Whatever Comes

"There is no force equal to a woman determined to rise." - W.E.B. Dubois

What about you? What is it that makes you tick? Are you being your true self when working around your colleagues or do you have to pretend to be someone else just to keep peace with your coworkers? I find it interesting watching women navigate the somewhat treacherous waters surrounding men at work. I thank God for the "good" men that do show up. Believe me, you will know the good men when you meet them. They prove their worth in the short and long run. It will be your allies who offer encouragement, show you a better way of working, and reject fake criticisms about you from other men. Numerous men have helped me out along my journey working in male-dominated environments. Being treated as an equal human being and having respect for another person's talents and knowledge is a standard worth striving toward for any of us. It's a mental and a moral thing. I needed their good vibes to counteract the bad vibes given off by men who had little to no respect for a woman working with or around them. I shudder when I think back to some of the situations that I encountered during my early days of working in male-dominated environments. The saying is true, "what doesn't break you only makes you stronger." Being strong is called for and very much needed in times of high mental stress. I was already mentally strong but I had to get stronger. Feminine strong.

How do you see yourself at work? Be honest. I do not pretend that all women are strong at the same time and in every situation. We are talking about our jobs, however. This is our livelihood, so let me ask the question again, "How do you see yourself at work?"

I am a woman who has always believed that if you set your mind to do something, you will eventually get it done if you want it bad enough. Will there be obstacles to overcome? Yes, we are talking about life and life has its challenges. No one escapes free and clear on that one. How any woman handles herself in a given situation speaks loudly to the men who work with her. If they know you to be the calm one in a storm, they will rely on you to be calm and steady even if they are freaking out (you will seldom, if ever, hear men speak about being nervous or anxious in front of you). If you are a panicked-stricken type of individual or one who gets upset, scared, or frustrated easily then chances are people (especially men) will turn and run the other way should a serious situation arise. We all want to know that we are in capable hands when the good times turn bad. What gets me is that no matter the personality type, most women working in male-dominated occupations are not considered mentally strong enough to lead a team to victory. This stems from that whole "too emotional" label many try to slap on all of us. Every woman cannot be a leader. This is true. Not every man can be an effective leader but most of them feel as if they can, especially over us. To be clear: a woman can lead a team. More women should lead male-dominated groups.

Leaders have an instinct to lead and they're born with it. A woman often has to learn her craft inside and out, backward and forward and prove time and time again that she is qualified just to be considered as a leader, *just to be considered as a leader.* Depending on a woman's race or ethnicity (the water in the pool of bias just got deeper), this proof can be exhaustingly unreasonable. This article highlights challenges faced by Black women in the workplace: Women in the Workplace: Black Women. Proving your abilities is not the issue. Proving one's ability beyond reason is the issue. Proving yourself is not a problem when you know your job (the whole up-and-down, backwards-and-forwards thing). The most important advice that I can give any woman is to have the confidence to show and tell others that you come with the goods in hand! Your capabilities are more than mere words!

In my earlier days working in male-dominated industries, I was given on-the-job training when I was hired. I will be the first to admit that everyone cannot be a trainer. Training is not in everyone's wheelhouse of abilities. Much of my training was stunted in the beginning due to the biases of two of my trainers. It is a terrible feeling to realize no one truly wants you as a member of their team because you are a woman. You feel like the last kid on the playground to be chosen for the team when the leaders choose the players they want to play with. Men compete with each other and teams compete too. It was automatically assumed the team with the female would not be able to pull their weight when it came to the workload. One of my coworkers made it clear how he felt when he said, "Why am I taking work away from a man who needs this job to support his family?"

I had to pause and think why he would say such a foolish thing. Did he refuse to believe I have wants and needs that also require an income? That I also needed a paycheck? According to him, since I was a woman, I should just get married or work as a nurse or something. I was not upset nor did I take what he said seriously, even though he meant it seriously. It was in that moment I knew that I was going to be one of the BEST workers this particular. company ever had. I did not know how or when it would happen, but I knew I could do it. Fortunately, he and his closest buddy at work were not the only men to train me. After much back and forth with bias issues, other men (who were more open and supportive of working with a woman) showed me what it would take to become an excellent worker in that department. That is what I sought after: excellence. There are times you have to make it happen despite who is trying to hold you back. Some people want to see you frustrated enough to quit. I liked my job and was determined to stay. Check out this article on stress and burnout from women who do not work in a male-dominated environment: Women Continuing To Face Alarmingly High Levels of Burnout, Stress In the "New Normal" of Work. Now think about the stressors you face on your job completely surrounded by men. How bad does it get for you and how do you deal with it? What do you do if quitting your job is not an option?

CHAPTER 3

Stand Your Ground

"I know what I bring to the table so believe me when I say that I am not afraid to eat alone."

Fear is a real thing and perception is everything, have you heard that before? If you are a woman who is fearful of what will happen (what can be said about you and your character and, in some instances, be physically done to you) when working with men, then you are missing out on some terrific jobs with generally good pay. I was never the type of woman who allowed fear of the unknown to stop me from doing what I wanted to do. Do I get afraid? Of course, I get afraid. At some point, we are all fearful of things we do not know the answer to or cannot see what is going to happen when we turn a certain corner. What I do know is that, overall, the fear that I projected in my mind never happened. Not even close. What makes this work less stressful is (1) you like the work and (2) if you still want to do it, you stay and overcome the challenges that can go along with being one of the best. In this instance, the best refers to a woman who speaks up against the biases that are shoved her way. I admit it can be quite intimidating to work around some men every day. I suppose if you are a woman who grew up with a lot of brothers then it may not be so bad because you generally have an idea of what it is like being around the male gender all the time. But putting up with the biases that people can throw at you while working is not something that anyone should have to get used to living with. Don't be fooled: the gossip mill in all-male circles is just as intense as the gossip mill containing all women. Men cannot wait to see which woman (if any) can even perform his job and heaven help us all when a woman shows up who can do the job better!

Before I continue, please note that I often choose the words "some" or "many" when referring to men. I do not want to use absolutes and suggest that all men are insecure, jealous, cutthroat, belittling or condescending in the way they interact with women on the job. Most men are very supportive, engaging, helpful, and respectful. A good team player truly comes to work to get the job done. It simply does not matter to this individual if their coworker is male or female. All that matters is whether he or she can pull their weight. I told you that you have to prove yourself. Proving yourself is not an issue when you know what you bring to the table. Your supportive male colleagues will be some of your best champions because they will speak of how good the quality of your work truly is. These allies tell of your capabilities and the value of your work when you are in the room, but especially when you are not. Do not worry about your haters. They are not there to testify truthfully to the quality of your work. The truth is haters will play down the quality of your work even when it is of superior quality. They will speak about every mistake no matter how minuscule. You must stay focused on doing your job and keep moving forward!

When I first started working in male-dominated professions, I found out some of the men took bets (gambling) to see how long I would last…can anyone say "appearance bias?" I suppose I did not look like someone who would work in those particular occupations (whatever that means). Two or three days on the job was as long as most of them gave me. These days, the bias towards me is considerably low. Are there still issues that I deal with from time to time? Yes, as long as people with bad intent walk the Earth, there will be contentions to deal with. These contentions are low in number and severity now compared to past times. They are rare, but they still happen. Be prepared and stay encouraged. When you know what to do and how to handle a situation, nothing seldom takes you out of your peaceful state of being. I work in peace with my coworkers…even the persons who do not like me (shame on them because I'm wonderful)! I am a Bias Breaking Beauty and you can be one too! I can show you how to manage biases the more time we spend getting to know one another. The time you waste not dealing with bias on the job is time you will never ger back.

CHAPTER 4.

Have No Fear

There are times when a meeting can lead to a spirited debate. Some topics that come up for discussion can cause strong emotional reactions. What I really mean to say is the conversation can get heated and intense. The conversational choice of words can often be loud and direct when people demand to get their point across and want everyone to hear it. For some reason, loudness is often connected to a better understanding of a situation, but I do not get the correlation. This intensity can make a woman nervous/anxious, especially if her world is quiet and organized. Not all women to be clear, but hearing men raise their voices to one another (or even to you) can make for an uncomfortable situation. For other women, getting loud is no problem at all. They are more than willing to reciprocate. This can be troublesome for new employees because they have not caught on to the company culture and do not exactly know what is happening at work. Intimidation is a real factor for women working in male-dominated occupations. Keep your guard up if you are a woman who tends to

11

speak her own truth. Fear is not an enemy unless it stops you from saying what you know to be true. I do believe when organizations listen to their female employees and seek their advice, those organizations do better from both a cultural and financial standpoint than companies who continually have a male-only frame of reference when making decisions. Just because a person is loud doesn't make them smart. Even the smart ones sometimes miss the mark, which becomes your opportunity to show your skillset. You have a good mind so use it. If you are fearful of every person who shows you their biases, then the buzzards will start to circle your body ready for the feast. Don't get eaten alive!

I have found that being loud doesn't get a woman's point across any better than using her natural tone of voice. I can hear men go ballistic with one another trying to make the other man see his point of view. Adding another loud voice to the mix generally doesn't help the situation. Often, it is the calmer head that prevails anyway. A woman should have her argument solid and draw her line in the sand (set a boundary on how you will be spoken to) rather than even attempt to speak over shouting men. While most men do not perceive their behavior as emotional (because boys will be boys), it is the woman who will be labeled as the emotional one if we get loud! I truly believe some men raise their voices thinking it will naturally make women go into the fetal position and back down or, better yet, never question or confront them to begin with. Do you know this type of woman? How do you respond to male-pattern loudness?

One last thing: You work in a male-dominated profession so you knew being outnumbered by the opposite sex was par for the course. Did you have a strategy in place for dealing with any coworkers who try to steal your ideas and claim them as their own?

A strategy for dealing with coworkers who talk over you in meetings, making you essentially unheard and unseen? Never allow anyone to force your hand or have you submit to something that you truly do not want to do. Going along to get along with others only works if everyone agrees to the same thing, good or bad. If you do not agree, speak up! It is almost like the saying, "You can get with this or you can get with that." Please choose wisely. Women pay a heavy price when we do not listen to our inner selves and join forces with intentions we do not totally support. Regardless of whether you are a new hire or have years of experience on the job, there will always be some men and women who will question your ability and your expertise. I already told you there will be coworkers who will try to make you believe you are not as good as you are. Every woman must know her worth and that her value is HIGH!

Connect with me on social and take the ColorDegree Voice Assessment to see what color your voice is at work:

FACEBOOK:

https://www.facebook.com/stephanie.myers.182940/

Join my new (private) FB group, Bias Breaking Beauty https://www.facebook.com/groups/biasbreakingbeauty

INSTAGRAM:

https://www.instagram.com/biasbreakingbeauty/

CHAPTER 5.

You Are Enough

Have you ever doubted your ability? Have you ever questioned whether you have what it takes to get the job done? At some point, many women have found themselves asking that inner question. No matter the job, the task at hand, or in our personal lives, this question undoubtedly springs into action when we are about to make a shift in our lives or about to enter into a new circumstance that requires just a little more thought to be put into it. This is the same inner question that stops many women from opening the door of opportunity. What stops many of us from opening the door of opportunity? The answer generally is this door requires us to do something different from what we are used to doing. Please do not allow a familiar job to prevent you from finding more peace, joy, and, should I dare say…happiness with a new job. I have heard if you love what you do then it doesn't feel like work. I believe this to be true even though I have not experienced it yet in my own life. I pray I get to find out for myself. I also pray that for you. Now, let's make it happen.

Women are smart. Women are smart enough and we have what it takes to be triumphant in reaching our goals. Whatever it is that a woman doesn't know, she will learn. Women can command a cruise ship, fly an airplane, or be on the next trip to the space station if that is our desire! Let us not forget about being a CEO or President (of a Fortune 500 organization or a country). We possess qualities that often go overlooked in the workplace. I have learned to be my own cheerleader. I seldom wait to be recognized for a job well done. Recognition may never come my way if I wait on another person to tell the truth or do the right thing! Use your voice to toot your own horn. It is only natural to question your ability at times. When you know your craft inside and out, questioning your ability will fade into oblivion once you have proven yourself. You know you have what it takes. Do not allow someone questioning your abilities to hold you back, especially if that individual cannot do the job either! Neither allow a mistake to determine your fate. You have what it takes to work in a male-dominated environment so make the most of it. Don't allow fear or making a mistake become your stumbling block.

Here's a quick example to prove my point: I made a terrible mistake one day at work that required me to redo the job and waste valuable time and effort. I really hate wasting time and effort in doing something! Needless to say, I had to start the task all over again. This caused a delay in processing time and put everyone else behind in doing their work (waiting on me to get it right). Two thoughts occurred to me at that moment: (1) I could have become so guilt-ridden for making a mistake that I lost all confidence in my capabilities (I was truly getting the hang of things at this point but I wanted to be one of *the best*) or (2), I could have allowed the jokes some of the men said about me rattle my thinking to the point that I did question whether I could be as good as some of them… let alone be one of the greatest among them! My inner voice started repeating the same question over and over again: "Do you have what it takes to do this job?" I would say to myself, "Men can naturally do this or men can do that job very well, but what can I do?" Answer: Anything I want. Men make mistakes on the job. I've seen it and so have many of you. They make mistakes and some of them try to hide them. An honest man will admit when he has made an error. I hate it when a woman makes the same mistake and some men treat it like it is the end of the world! Don't allow yourself to be fooled.

It is going to be very difficult for any woman to stand up and remain standing if she does not believe that she has what it takes to succeed. Mindset is everything when working in a male-dominated environment. Women can do the same job as men, thanks to technology. In many instances, technology has made life easier for all of us. As far as I can tell, the only thing that men have over women is the ability to lift heavier objects with their bodies. Since the age of automation, who is lifting something really heavy with their bodies all day, every day? Brainpower and various tools help level the playing field. Women have the same intelligence as men so the field is more level from an academic standpoint than ever before. That's a good thing. I realize there are "other issues" women face, but that is where support for gender diversity comes into play. Women working in maintenance and other departments have tools which help them stay on top of their game. Women can and do leap over hurdles day after day after day. I do believe the phrase "it's a man's job" will completely disappear as more and more women enter the job market and come to expect a level playing field. I encourage every woman to apply for any job that interests her. If you know how to perform three out of the five or six requirements for that job, go for it! You can learn the other steps once you get the job! Don't wait until you meet all six of the requirements (why are we doing this anyway?). A man doesn't wait...he moves if he has only two skills out of six because that man knows he will learn the rest once he gets the job!

CHAPTER 6.

Flaming Hot

"Some women fear the fire, others become it." – R. H. Sin

It is wonderful when everybody agrees on the very same thing. It generally makes the process operate a lot smoother. What if you are put in a situation where the men perform a job one way, but you like doing it the opposite way? I had to face that very situation. This was a simple task that turned into a big ordeal. When all things are equal there should not be any disagreement, right? Problems can arise when something new is entered into the program. Picture this: All the men start this particular job on the right side. I found the right side to be more of a challenge so I would perform the job from the left side. Since both sides of the container were equal, it did not matter which side I started on… it was the same. The individual in charge of our team (a man) directed me to start the job from the right side (this is the way the men do it, after all). I explained to him why I did not like to start from the right and that it truly made no difference in this instance. I mean, this had nothing to do with a safety issue or anything of that nature so it did not matter which side was started first. You already know what happened… a heated disagreement ensued. Full disclosure: this man was known for wanting everything done his way; there was no wiggle room to do it any other way but his. The only difference was in his tone of voice. I never heard him speak to a man the way he would yell at me. Now, at this point, a decision had to be made…should I continue to do it my way (comfortable) or submit to doing the job his way (uncomfortable)? I chose my way, but before I did it my way there had to be a meeting of the minds. I stopped the project right there and went to talk with our immediate supervisor. I calmly explained what was going on with the project. The supervisor came out to the job site area, looked at what I was talking about, had a few words with the man in charge of the team, and proceeded to inform me to go back to work and do it my way. The job was completed with success. The man in charge of the team was angry (furious to tell the truth). He did not take it out on me that day. I truly believed he liked yelling at me because he thought it made me nervous. He waited to yell another day about something else. Then he stopped yelling altogether and started talking to me. Years later, he informed me that he was just trying to make me a better worker. No, I do not understand that type of logic and neither should you. From that one incident and moving forward however, he learned that I would not be pushed around. A line was drawn in the sand.

I tell you this story so you can be aware that times will arise when the way a man does something is not the way a woman may want to do it. In this instance, it was not about proving my point over his, it was more about what worked best for me since I was the person doing the job. There will be times when people will try and push their ways of doing and thinking onto you. If a woman does not know any better or just wants to go-along-to-get-along, there will be fewer problems at work but at what cost to the woman…at what costs to you? If you can live with that, fine, I could not. I said something and, in this instance, I did something about it. You have to know your job well to challenge a team leader on any job. I knew my job and my capabilities. I knew them both well. I was not a new hire and I did not have to play the 'get along' game. It did not bother me that my coworker was angry nor did it interest me. If I can work with you, that is great. If I cannot work with you, so be it. I'm fine either way. One thing is certain: I would not be pressured into doing a job I was uncomfortable with doing. Doing the job in an uncomfortable position could possibly have become a safety issue. Every woman must be willing to stand up for herself. Men look to see who will stand up or who will just do whatever they say to do. Some men will tell you anything just to see how you will react to what is said or done. Most of the time work is completed in the same manner. When a difference or a change is given the spotlight, people (not just men) can get a little testy in their behavior. Change of any kind can be fearful for people. *Be the fire* if fire is what is called for. Learn how to stand up and speak up for yourself.

CHAPTER 7.

Decision Makers

"Women belong in all places where decisions are being made…it shouldn't be that women are the exception." – Ruth Bader Ginsburg.

I have been involved in many meetings with male coworkers and the overall vibe in the place is that men run the show. Granted, if you are newly hired, until you get the lay of the land there may be a few meetings where your voice is silent. One reason for this is a new hire is still figuring out the who, what, when, where, and how of each meeting and trying to make sense of it all. Once you learn what's going on and who each player in the game is, it will become imperative for you to speak up and add value to the conversation. Add information that will help the group, not just fluff to hear yourself talk. No one is interested in that. Keep in mind that most men think they are always right…until they aren't! This is yet another reason why knowing your job inside and out, up and down, backward and forwards, is a must! When a mistake is made, you are the one to correct it.

I want to add this caveat regarding a woman belonging in meetings and making decisions with men. Depending on the man, he may laugh at just about anything you suggest (think microaggression). This can often be a sign of him trying to intimidate you. If he laughs, then there is a possibility that others will laugh at you too or at least give a sheepish grin. Some people will always be followers. Keep making your suggestions and have a good reason as to why your plan of action is valid. Improve your argument about why your suggestion is best and try to overlook the clowns in the room. I know this is easier said than done but don't fall into the emotional trap game!

Here are three tips if your suggestions are ignored or laughed at during a meeting:

1.) *Validate your point with facts: Respond firmly with evidence that supports your position. You are the professional in the room so remain calm and maintain a steady but sure tone of voice.*

2.) *Seek allies: I haven't written much on the subject of allies, be they male or female, but allies are essential to helping any woman working in a male-dominated environment. Allies are persons that you TRUST. Tell him or her what happened during a meeting and how you felt about it. Normally, they can suggest alternatives on how to better perform a job, handle a situation, and why you should not feel bad about yourself in the face of laughter. To be honest, the leader of the meeting should not allow laughter towards anyone's ideas if that leader wants people to freely contribute. Not all leaders are good leaders.*

3.) *Empower your mind: Here is where your self-confidence springs forth. We all face setbacks at some point in our lives. If your suggestion was dismissed or laughed at during a meeting this time around, it does not mean that it will be dismissed or laughed at during the next meeting. At this point, you must remind yourself of all your achievements, hard work, and skillset that you bring to the table. You are not there by accident. Be your own cheerleader. Yes, some groups are more difficult to tackle than others and it will take more time to conquer some types of bias vs another type. Again, the leader of the group should be able to make*

I have found that women bring different ways of thinking and doing to the table that works just as well, if not better, than what is currently being implemented. Supportive men will think about what is said and will state whether this is a good idea, plan, or objective that can and will be implemented. You can trust their opinion on such matters. Other men will knock down every idea you suggest. Don't let that slow you down; keep moving forward. Over time (and it will take time), what you say will carry as much weight as any man in the room. More importantly, back up what you say with as much proof as possible! Proof is always better than mere hearsay or speculation. You are not one of the guys; you are one of the great women who work in a male-dominated industry and you are succeeding! Always remember that if you doubt your ability the men will sense it and start doubting you too.

CHAPTER 8

Permission Granted

"Speak the truth even if your voice shakes."

I am convinced for most women, working in a male-dominated environment is not something they aspire to do. Not even a little bit and that's okay. For women who currently work in male-dominated jobs and for the women who may come in the future to work in a male-dominated environment… listen up. It is my expressed belief that unless you are confident in who you are as a woman and confident in your capabilities, work of this nature will become a grueling process for you. You can learn a job and learn to perform it well. If you are not emotionally strong and sure of what you will and will not put up with, working in a nearly all-male environment can turn into a nightmare. Some work environments will try and rob you of your sanity. Many will question your ability and judgment at every turn. This is true even when you know the job better than they do! When those times happen, firmly remind the individual that this is not your first rodeo. Essentially, a woman must know which battles to fight and which ones to simply let go. I say this after much trial and error on my behalf. Some disagreements with a colleague, I should have just let it go and moved on. "It did not take all that," as my mother used to say. But then again, she also said, "Things happen just as they should have [happened]." Go figure.

Peace of mind is a wonderful thing! Many disagreements between you and a coworker can be settled without any grief or strife. People learn to compromise and come to an understanding that one way of doing something is simply better than another. A team works together to reach a specific goal no matter who has the better idea. The main thing is to do your part and carry your own bucket. When you know deep down that you are a member of the team, you can sit at the table reassured that a woman is there on purpose and not by accident! If you find yourself being the only woman in a meeting stacked full of men, think of these things:

1.) You are one of the smartest people in the room. Even a dumb man will act like he is smarter than you simply because you are the female.
2.) Sit up straight in your chair and make eye contact with every man in the room. This type of body language supports the fact that you are qualified to be at the table with them.
3.) When you are challenged (expect it), state the facts and leave emotions out of it. Ideas, plans, and objectives to be implemented require clear and concise instructions for a plan of action, not emotions.
4.) Gather some feedback from people you know and trust. A true friend or ally will be honest and tell you what worked well and what suggestions fell short of the mark. You can take constructive criticism, can't you?

Organizations need a variety of ways to look at executing a plan. One way of doing something may not be the only way or the best way. Women help provide variety and a broader perspective in many cases. Your ideas matter.

CHAPTER 9

Voice Control

"Women have power over themselves, not over men." – Mary Shelley

It has always seemed strange to me when women want to focus on changing men and their attitudes instead of first working on changing themselves, i.e., using our voices and taking action to make change occur. The battle to change a man's way of thinking can be a lift too heavy to perform in the beginning. It is much easier to control your mind than someone else's. This book is about finding what reasons are holding you back from reaching your full potential in front of your male coworkers. What is stopping you from expressing your thoughts and ideas at work? Remember the question in the first chapter…" *Do you, as a woman, speak up or hold your peace in the presence of men*?" You only have the power to control the way you respond to whatever anyone says or does to you. A man is going to do and act as he sees fit in many instances. I feel this has something to do with women being viewed as the "weaker sex." The word weak tends to make many believe they can just tell us what to do at work and we just blindly go ahead and do it. Forget that women often have a better and generally more efficient way of dealing with a situation. The fact is anyone can be wrong. After all, no one is perfect. There can be more ways than one to reach an objective. Thank goodness for male allies at work because gender does not matter to this type of man. As long as a woman can do the job and do it correctly, this type of man has no problem working with us or for us. Your work will speak for itself. Results matter. Do your own thinking and take responsibility for your own decisions and actions. This statement rings true for both the rank-and-file woman, dressed in her company uniform, and women dressed in business attire working in the C-suites of major organizations. Be in charge of your own life at work and play. It is proven to us practically every day that women move mountains when and if the mountain needs to be moved. Are you willing? Are you capable of using the biased stones thrown at you to strengthen your own resolve to keep moving forward? The only action that you should be interested in taking is one that allows your dreams to SOAR!

Here is one of my favorite stories of men standing up for me: My team and I were at lunch. Seated at the table are three men and myself preparing to eat. The subject comes up regarding (a) what time are we going to start the next project, (b) how long do we think this will take and (c) what person should be in charge of getting it done correctly the first time around? There were contractors in the area who needed our help completing their job. Of course, the men bantered back and forth amongst themselves when one of them looked at me and said, "Hey Steph, would you be interested in helping the contractors after lunch?" Full disclosure: I had no idea what was required of this particular job. I don't think anyone knew until the contractors came. I accepted and we began working after lunch.

The contractors needed material moved an inch here and an inch there while working on repairing a support beam. Using huge equipment to move product an inch here or there is not as simple as it seems when the material needs it to be in one exact spot and be stabilized. It is easy to miss the mark and have to start over. The distance is overwhelmingly short. Fortunately, the job was completed with success and within time limitations. The contractors complimented me on my skillset while in the presence of my team. The contractors stated they had never witnessed anyone with such a touch that could lift or lower their material to the exact spot they needed (on the first attempt) and keep it steady while they did their work. The job generally took much longer to complete. They seemed thrilled and were astounded when they realized I was a woman! It is times like this…times when even the outside world has to recognize your skillset and acknowledge it, that shuts the mouth of every man who dared question whether I was good enough. I was more than capable. I was one of the best!

As we strive to break the back of bias within our respected industries, it will be on our shoulders to do what is necessary to draw attention to the challenges we face. Silence will not get this particular objective accomplished. It is our singular and collective voices together that bring attention to our plight. I am a "#biasbreakingbeauty" and you can be one too! We can speak our truth and change how women are treated at work. Fighting bias on the job is one thing, but it is nothing if we cannot speak up for ourselves and take action! Take the ColorDegree Voice Assessment found on my social media pages and see what color of voice you tend to use at work. When a woman understands why she acts or reacts the way she does, true change begins to take shape. Permit yourself to use your voice. Understand your "why" and take the ColorDegree Voice Assessment now:

Meta: https://www.facebook.com/groups/biasbreakingbeauty

IG: https://www.instagram.com/biasbreakingbeauty/

Website: https://biasbreakingbeauty.com/

CHAPTER 10

Does It Matter?

"Our lives begin to end the day we become silent about things that matter." –

Dr. Martin Luther King, Jr.

I am sure Dr. King was frying bigger fish when he spoke those words. Still, the message is solid even for women who work alongside a group of men. Should you choose to stay and endure, the time will come when you will have to speak your truth to one, if not all, of your male colleagues, salaried and non-salaried alike. Work is work until the dynamic changes. The change occurs when a woman enters the circle and is recognized for being a true worker and quite possibly, a true leader.

Take heart, fellow warriors, it is not all doom and gloom. I can attest to that fact. If it starts out difficult, for most of us, those days will pass so long as women do not back down to pressure. Misogyny is a beast to contend with but people will come to know you for the woman that you are…smart, kind, no-nonsense, funny, assertive-when-need-be…use whatever adjectives speak to your personality. Men talk and (if they're honest) will tell one another which woman might make it and which woman will not. Men will give you a fair shake so long as you are pulling your share of the workload. I do find encouragement in the way more women step up and decide that male-dominated environments are just that…male-dominated. Our thoughts should be acknowledged and this is why it is so important for us to open our mouths and be heard. It is a terrible thing to hear someone say, "You should have said something," in a meeting when the only solution decided upon was not a very good solution to the problem at all. Women hold a wealth of knowledge and we should not be afraid to share it. Speak up if you have a solution. Even if your suggestion is not taken seriously at that particular time, keep speaking. A breakthrough will come simply because no one person or group holds the answer to everything. Do you agree or disagree?

I realize some of my suggestions are more easily said than done. Healing takes time if you have ever experienced bias on the job. So does finding your voice and speaking up. Perhaps you have tried to share your thoughts in times past and always got interrupted, talked over, or not taken seriously. Psychological safety is not something that every company pays attention to when protecting their female employees. I have experienced incidents with male colleagues that caused me to speak up because there was no other way around it. Was I ladylike in all my conversations? No, but I have always been respectful, even when I spoke with a stern and direct tone. I have never considered being assertive a negative when it comes to being a woman or a lady. I wear it as a badge of honor the way men do. I am human…I am a woman. Being assertive in my tone of voice, when necessary, makes people realize that I am not joking when I am talking to them. Everything is not a joke. As a woman working in a male-dominated industry, you simply cannot run to the human resources office about every incident (only the truly inappropriate ones). In some work environments, you will have to speak up and tell the individual or group directly what you mean right then and there. It's called "handling the situation." Deal with it and handle it! I can help you with circumstances around standing your ground.

I help women not only find their voice but use their voices without fear of being intimidated. Knowing how to respond to a given situation is a powerful tool to have in your arsenal against biased behavior. I help women manage the biases that leaves so many of us feeling like we are the weakest link, the invisible woman, or simply someone incapable of doing the job correctly. I listen to what you say is happening and show you why you're more than the "one" men simply have to put up with! Not only will you feel liberated to do your job to its maximum best, but the trauma that experiencing bias puts on our minds and bodies has to stop! You can learn to express your thoughts while growing your self-esteem. 'Prove them wrong' is a great mantra to declare moving forward. Intimidation will become a show-stopper if you allow it to become a giant at work. If not speaking up and holding your own at work is an issue for you, contact me and together we will figure out what works best for you. Just like every woman is unique, so are the types of biases that we each encounter on our jobs. Here is a quick peek at just a few types. See if you recognize any of them Implicit Vs Explicit Bias: Differences, Effects and Steps To Tackle These Biases. Now, what are you going to do about it?

CHAPTER 11.

What Will He Say?

Have you ever felt like the invisible woman at work? I have and I believe many of you know that feeling too. During my early days of working in male-dominated environments, the meetings were held daily and, of course, a couple of men would not let anyone else get a word in to respond to a question, give an update if something happened during the shift, etc. I was overlooked many times. Once I knew what my job entailed and was qualified enough to perform it correctly and safely, I wanted to speak and give all the details that happened during my shift. In one particular meeting, before anyone had a chance to speak and tell their version of a particular incident, I spoke first and gave valuable information. I also waited to see if there were any questions to follow. The look on everyone's face made me think they were going to laugh but they didn't. I believe the group was just shocked to hear me speak and talk like I knew what I was doing… because I did! From that moment on, I was no longer overlooked or invisible to anyone.

My point? If we, as a major part of the workforce, do not gather within ourselves the ability to use our voices for the betterment of our gender, our organization, businesses, and communities, who else will? You never know what the person sitting beside you or

"

behind you is going to say… what if it is something ridiculous and you have a better idea? Let your voice be heard and understood. Whenever you do that, your teammates will know that you are not there to just collect a paycheck and go home. You participate and stay involved with matters concerning your group just as much as anyone else. You have value too and your voice matters. Little by little this becomes a known fact to all, even to the people who speak most often in any setting. The thing that gets recognized is you now have the will and determination to speak. Speak no matter who is in the room and share your point of view, especially when asked to do so. Only fools laugh at a great idea that is not their own. Do not allow anyone to claim your idea as theirs and steal your thunder! That happens more often than people realize.

CHAPTER 12.

Being Afraid Will Not Save You

"Fear has torment"- Rev Bob White (and Jesus)

One of the worst emotions to have and hold onto is fear. Even worse is the fact that what we imagine will happen, oftentimes does not happen at all! We have wasted our energy on thoughts that will never occur in our lives. Of course, fear and torment don't end with just our thoughts. Over time, fear spreads within our bodies and we can end up jeopardizing our health. How many times have you been to the doctor and the doctor asks you, "How much stress is in your life?" or something to that effect? We all know about stress and seldom does anyone refer to it as being good. We shift it from our mind directly to our body.

No woman wants to add more problems to her life, yet stress, if not dealt with, will ultimately take a toll on your physical well-being. Woman, tell the truth, how do you feel when you are overlooked for a promotion that you know you were qualified to have? Do you like being considered the "weakest link" on the team simply because you are a woman? What about having your decisions questioned at every turn like you are new to the job? From a woman working in a leadership position to the employee who scans her timecard in and out for work, we suffer bias in many forms. We have to use our voices to bear witness to these types of abuses and work together to stop it completely. Yes, stop it and not simply lower the number

33

of instances bias shows up. Lowering the number of instances is a start, but we must not settle with a lower number. To eradicate and eliminate bias is the top goal. Women must work together to stop the biases associated with working in male-dominated environments. I am thankful for the #MeToo Movement. A floodlight should be placed on sexual harassment and dehumanizing behavior but let's be clear: any type of bias against women whether physical violence or the spoken word is not to be tolerated. Before a man gets to physically harassing a woman (up to and including her being raped on the job), a statement (words) of some type has been made that egregiously crossed the line of work-related conduct. What if the man says he was "only joking" by the words that came out of his mouth? As a woman, you can take a joke, right? Note how the incident makes you feel in that moment…are you laughing aloud or cringing inside? If you cannot combat the bias right then, keep a journal and write it down if it makes you cringe. Misogyny can be so subtle and disguised so well that it is naturally played off as a joke by men when a woman seeks accountability for biased behavior. Bias is no laughing matter and everything that a man says to you is not funny. Men know this to be true. Don't be fooled into thinking that condescending statements or hostile language are okay and just part of your job. It is not okay because you are worthy of the same respect that you show him. Staying silent only allows for biased behavior to continue and a bad situation can always get worse! When it gets worse, you do not like coming to work, your mind can place you in a state of depression, and the physical toll that all this stress is wreaking on your body can be overwhelming. Do you get headaches/migraines just thinking about some of the misogynistic people working at your job? Fear will cost you more than you are willing to pay. Deal with the bias on your job whether it is directed toward you or any other female coworker. As women in a specific work environment such as ours, we have to stand up for one another. First, learn to take care of yourself, and over time you will be strong enough to help support other women in the workplace. This is how we change the face of bias from being perceived as "normal behavior" in one's thinking to calling it out for what it is – a close-minded, prejudicial, and downright patriarchal mindset! We do not have to deal with this type of malignancy in our lives. We are more valuable as a collective than we give ourselves credit. What we bring to our jobs cannot be downplayed by anyone. You are more than your job so biased attitudes cannot rule the work environment – no matter how small an incident is portrayed to be.

CHAPTER 13.

Microaggressions

"Life is not easy for any of us. But what of that? We must have perseverance and, above all, confidence in ourselves. We must believe we are gifted for something and that this thing must be attained." – Marie Curie

A microaggression is often an unintentional discrimination against members of a marginalized group. A remark made by someone sincerely meaning no harm in what he or she just said, yet for the person hearing that remark, harm was done. A statement like "You speak so well" can be meant as a compliment but for the marginalized individual hearing this, to me, it sounds more like "I speak well for whom (a black woman or just the African-American race in general)? Many marginalized people hear microaggressions on a daily basis. It is now up to us to bring attention to this macro issue and put it to rest, especially on our jobs. This is but one example of a microaggression that I did not deal with correctly on my job. Yes, the person who said this microaggression truly meant no harm. In fact, she meant it as a compliment. How could she have known the statement just made was from old stereotypical slave tropes passed down from generation to generation? I found this Forbes article so interesting in helping me to realize just how prevalent microaggressions are and how detrimental they can be to an exposed person's mental and physical well-being that I wanted to share it with you, <u>Why There Is Nothing "MICRO" About Microaggressions</u>. I did not respond to this comment like I should have. I should have politely informed her that what she said was a microaggression. Then, I should have explained what a microaggression was and how the use of it harms people like myself. What did I do instead? I let it go and didn't say a word (because she meant no harm, right?). Wrong! Everything listed above I should have done. First, is to inform the person about their comment so this type of malignancy is not spread to someone else. Second, to speak up for what I know is right and add value to my own self-worth. After all, I went to school just like the majority of people working at my job. What was I supposed to sound like when I spoke?

Lesson learned. I believe one of the main reasons so many microaggressions permeate the air is that too few individuals address it when it happens to them. The person hearing the microaggression does not speak up and the person saying this foolishness does not know, in most cases, that he or she has said anything wrong at all! It only stops when we decide to do better, to want better for one another.

Microaggressions are exclusionary statements that often leave victims feeling they are somehow different and not like other people. You are inferior in some shape or fashion. It's pure discrimination packaged in a more subtle and indirect way of speaking. Unintentional or not, comments that make anyone (women in general and women of color in particular) feel less than equal are comments that will not and should not be tolerated any longer. I realize this comes at a time when it appears the whole world wants to speak and share their opinion, but what you say to a person matters. This statement is true at work or at home. How are you using your voice when it comes to any comment that makes you feel less worthy than your coworkers? Now is not the time to be quiet because silence is not a strategy!

CHAPTER 14.

MY FAITH

She considereth a field, and buyeth it: with the fruit of her hands she planteth

a vineyard. -- Proverbs 31:16

I do not want to give the impression that managing biased attitudes at work is easy. It is hard and requires a confident and strategically-thinking woman to not allow biased attitudes to get the best of her. You have to remain confident in yourself and your abilities. Your mindset is key. The main way I stay focused on myself and not what is happening on the job is through the teachings of Jesus Christ. No, I'm not about to get religious on you but I do want to share with you how I maintained perspective in the face of biased attitudes at work. On numerous occasions, my work environment became so hostile that I had no choice but to follow the chain of command and tell senior-level leadership i.e., the plant manager, what was happening within my department. My faith in Christ is the glue that held everything together. When you are outnumbered in gender it can become easy to just "stay in your small space and not make any waves." I could not maintain that way of thinking, living, working and neither should you. You will have to have someone or something to hold onto should a storm arise in your life. A storm of some type will come, if not at work, then at home, but it will come. Having someone to share the most intimate details concerning my job and who will not let me down in the long run, is my faith in Christ. Whoever you believe (or not) is up to you.

I pray your ship holds together whenever the storms of life pass your way and you get thrown against the rocks. You will need a sure foundation then.

Having leadership on any level, but in my instance senior-level leadership, who would listen to my concerns and then speak with the department head to get a much broader perspective of what was happening within the department was crucial. It is just as vital today as in times past. More than deciding the outcome of an issue, senior-level leadership should attempt to bring cohesiveness to the unit. My concern has come up to the top brass so a judgment (policy) call has to be made regarding right and wrong behavior. Oftentimes, women are too afraid to voice our concerns to management for fear of (you tell me what is stopping you from using your voice to correct wrongdoing). Right there, the reason that just entered your mind is why you and I must connect and eradicate this madness called bias once and for all! Bias against women, particularly women working in male-dominated professions, is a prejudice that none of us have to deal with yet we do. For whatever reason, women have "put up with" being made to feel unsafe in speaking our opinions, perpetuated as unskilled when we know exactly what we are doing and, in some instances, treated completely inferior to our male counterparts. If bias has reared its ugly head in any of its various forms, let's connect and together we can decapitate this monster once and for all!

Women, together we are a community of support and a place of refuge. No one truly knows what we experience on a day-to-day basis simply because of our work environment. I am a Bias Breaking Beauty and soon you will be one too! Together, we are a force to be reckoned with! Here are a few ways women can help one another: 6 Ways Women Can Champion Each Other At Work. After all, there are enough of us that we should not be divisive regarding biased behavior. If I support you and you support me, plus the fact that women make up a large segment of the working class in most countries, we can no longer be denied our hopes and dreams. If your desire is to be a stay-at-home mom then go for it! If your goal is to be the best heavy equipment operator, 4-star general, or the 54th CEO of a Fortune 500 firm, go for it! Women can do it. Women are doing it!

If you want it, make certain, because sacrifices have to be made no matter the occupation or job title.

SUMMARY

As more women enter into the job market, the search for higher-paying jobs are needed. Men still make more money per job (when compared to the jobs women perform) even though the jobs are similar in nature, i.e., the gender pay gap. We celebrate women achieving and coming so far throughout history just to be faced with societal expectations of gender-based jobs today. For the women who decide to work in a male-occupied industry, obstacles remain to this day (to our shame). I encourage women to work in whatever job makes them happy (a blessing). Specifically, one that pays your bills and you have money left over at the end of the month. Many of those jobs can be found in male-dominated occupations. For those of you who work these types of jobs, you can and will thrive in your area of expertise. Hang in there. Learning how to maneuver around whatever obstacle stands in your way will help you stay and not get too frustrated, upset or depressed when working with your male colleagues. I mentioned biases faced when working with majority men but bias can also show up when working with female superiors too. That is another book altogether. I mentioned some basic obstacles that I encountered with a few of my coworkers/management. Many of my teammates were a delight to work with and we are friends to this day. I chose to keep my job since I do like working in male-dominated environments. If you desire to work in a male-dominated occupation or remain working in this type of environment, here are a few simple techniques to

41

help keep your peace of mind until you gather the know-how to speak up:

- Remember to breathe. Whenever you feel frustrated and start getting anxious, take some deep breaths and focus your mind on something pleasant. Unclench your jaws and relax your muscles. This technique eases tension. Don't allow tension to build up.
- Depending on your job, play some soft music to calm yourself (or if hard rock does it for you, go for it). The point here is to gather your thoughts and not blow up!
- If you are not into the music scene, finish that book you started and never finished, or take a boxing class and let it all out! Whenever I find myself getting frustrated, I always read inspirational quotes that reinforce what a strong woman I am. I now listen to inspirational words on YouTube.
- No matter your job: Go to the bathroom, splash some water on your face and return to center (home base for your thoughts). The water is cool and refreshing giving you time to steady your mind and think about something good. Think about things that you are grateful for in your life. This brings a smile and supplies a quick break away from the crap that is going on with your job.

These are simple ways to calm your thinking and not stay upset all day. They help keep you steady and in control of your thoughts until you learn how to speak up and defend yourself and your position. Be on the lookout for a companion journal that supports this book, I'm working on it now. It will help you reflect on what pains you the most about working alongside your male coworkers and how it is possible to find peace within yourself while dealing with anything that comes your way. Change the way you handle a situation and stop trying to change the mindset of your colleagues (cause some of them may never change how they feel about working with a woman!) Remember to take the ColorDegree Voice Assessment and see what color of voice you are currently using to say what you mean when speaking to others.

I listed some of the biases that I faced while working in male-dominated professions. I purposefully left out some of the harsher biases so that most women working in male-dominated fields could relate to the examples I used earlier in my writing. Women deal with biases on many levels when working with men. All most of us want is to simply do our jobs and be recognized for the effort that we put forth. I did not want to overwhelm you with the sheer volume of experiences that I have encountered while doing my job. If you think bias between one coworker and another is difficult to manage, wait for the second book where I discuss bias among leadership and how to overcome those traps without having your heart turn cold. You can overcome the biases that haunt you. You no longer have to smile and swallow every condescending statement that flows your way. I will show you how to manage bias but you must realize that you will need your voice to make it happen! Check me out on social media and prepare to stop the pain you thought would never go away. Bias is a prejudice that has to go away sooner rather than later!

Remember, Silence is not a Strategy!
Until next time ladies,

Stephanie

***LET'S KEEP IN TOUCH!***

STEPHANIE MYERS – Your Bias Breaking Beauty #biasbreakingbeauty

Follow me:

FACEBOOK:
https://www.facebook.com/groups/biasbreakingbeauty

INSTAGRAM: https://www.instagram.com/biasbreakingbeauty/

Website: https://biasbreakingbeauty.com/

- Leave your email address for new announcements and "all about women" news!

AND COMING SOON:

My LinkedIn page: Stephanie Myers

My Podcast: Bias Breaking Beauty
Be sure an subscribe!